WHAT·DO·WE·KNOW
ABOUT  THE
AZTECS·?

JOANNA DEFRATES

PETER BEDRICK BOOKS
NEW YORK

First American edition published in 1993 by
Peter Bedrick Books
2112 Broadway
New York, NY 10023

Published by agreement with Simon & Schuster
Young Books, Hemel Hempstead, England

Library of Congress Cataloging-in-Publication Data
Defrates, Jeanne.
    What do we know about the Aztecs? /
Joanna Defrates. – 1st American ed.
    Includes index.
    Summary: An illustrated introduction to the history,
religion, customs, and eventual fate of the Aztecs.
    ISBN 0-87226-357-6
    1. Aztecs–Juvenile literature. [1. Aztecs.
    2. Indians of Mexico.]   I. Title.
    F1219.73.D44   1993   92-16997
972′.004974–dc20   CIP
                                         AC

Design: David West
            Children's Book Design

Illustrator: Rob Shone

Copy editor: Ros Mair

Photograph acknowledgements:
Akademische Druck-u. Verlagsanstalt, Graz: p9(b),
p31(b), p41(t); Biblioteca Apostolica Vaticana: p28(r);
The Bodleian Library: M.S. Arch. Selden. A.I. p14
(fol.71.R), p16(fol.61.R), p19(t)(fol.61.R), p20(t)(fol.60.R),
p20(b)(fol.61.R), p21(t)(fol.60.R), p21(b)(fol.65.R),
p23(b)(fol.70.R), p27(b)(fol.64.R) p32(fol.67.R),
p33(b)(fol.7.V), p39(t)(fol.64.R), p40(fol.46.R),
p41(b)(fol.64.R); Courtesy the Trustees of the British Museum:
cover p18, p27(t), p30; p31(t) E.T. Archive: p8, p9(t), p22,
p29(b), p38(t), p42; Werner Forman Archive: endpapers, p6,
p12, p13(b), p19(b), p23(t), p24(b), p26(b), p28(l), p29(t),
p33(t), p35(l), p38(l); Robert Harding Picture Library/G.A.
Mather: p34(t), /Museum Für Völkerkunde: p39(b); Historia
General: p13(t), p14(b), p15, p17(both), p35(t), p37, Museum
Für Völkerkunde, Vienna: p26(t); South American Pictures: p43(t);
TRIP/Andrew Gasson: p25, p34(b), /Richard Powers: p43(b).

Picture research: Jennie Karrach

Typeset by: Goodfellow & Egan, Cambridge

Printed and bound by: BPCC Hazell Books, Paulton
and Aylesbury, England

Endpapers: This sculpture is from Tenochtitlan and shows the
Feathered Serpent, the symbol of the god Quetzalcoatl.

· CONTENTS ·

WHO·WERE·THE·AZTECS?

About eight hundred years ago a wandering tribe entered the high plateau valley of the land we now call Mexico. They called themselves Mexica (*Mesheeca*) but we know them as Aztecs. They rose to become the strongest people in the valley. They called their land Anahuac or 'The Land between the Waters' and ruled from their city, Tenochtitlan. They saw themselves as the rightful heirs of the Toltecs, past rulers of the valley.

THE TRIBAL GOD

The Aztecs were led by their tribal god, Huitzilopochtli or 'The Humming Bird of the Left', who was a warrior god demanding human sacrifice. Priests carried an image of the god in their long journey to find a settled home. Forced to keep moving, they wandered for nearly two hundred years before their god allowed them to stop on a mosquito-infested island on a lagoon. An eagle sitting on a cactus eating a serpent would show them where to build their city. The eagle was a symbol of the sun who gave them life and the cactus stood for the human hearts the god needed to live.

THE AZTEC WORLD

PACIFIC OCEAN

EXPANSION AND CONQUEST

Tenochtitlan was founded in about 1325. For the next hundred years the Aztecs organized themselves and built their city of Tenochtitlan. It was divided into four main areas with sub-divisions for each group of families and craftsmen. As they lacked space and raw materials, the Aztecs traded with neighboring tribes and married into local noble families. Soon they were taking over their lands too. By 1500 they ruled the whole valley and Tenochtitlan was the center of a strong military power. Twenty years later they were invaded themselves.

AZTEC PEOPLE

The Aztecs were described by the Spanish as quite tall and well-proportioned with straight black hair, brown eyes and skin. They were fearless of death and very war-like, skillful and with quick understanding.

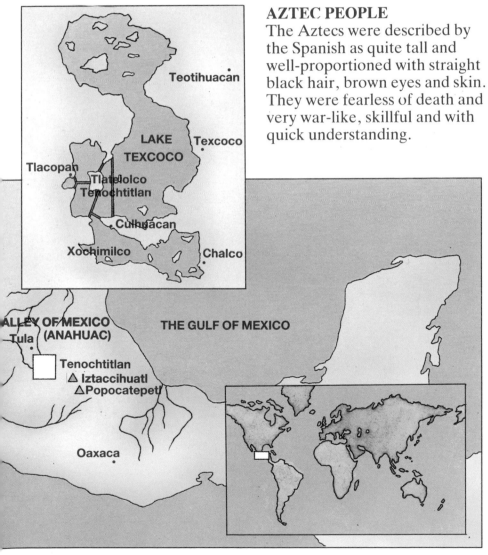

HOW DO WE KNOW?

1 Through archaeology – many Aztec sites have been excavated. It is 450 years since the collapse of the temples, and they are now about 23 feet to 26 feet below ground.

2 Codices have survived – the books of the Aztecs themselves (although many were destroyed, as they were considered to be the 'devil's works'.)

3 Books in Spanish and Nahuatl (the Aztec language) were written, after the invasion, about Aztec life and customs.

	AD 1200	1250	1300	1350	1400
VALLEY OF MEXICO	**1200** Aztecs enter the valley from the North.	**1250** Valley full of small tribal groups often fighting each other. Aztecs settle near Lake Texcoco.	**1325** Traditional date for the foundation of the city of Tenochtitlan. **1350** Swamps drained and causeways built with canals between them.	**1370** Tenoch, the Aztec priest-ruler, dies. Aztecs still under rule of Tepanecs who control the valley.	**1400** Tepanecs defeated. The Aztecs expand their territory and become rulers of the whole valley. All other tribes send them tribute. Rule by a military élite.
EUROPE	**1204** Fourth Crusade. **1215** Magna Carta signed.	**1250** Growth of power of the King in England.	**1314** Battle of Bannockburn. Scotland defeated England.	**1350** Black Death in Europe followed by economic collapse. Peasants Revolt in England.	**1415** Battle of Agincourt. Henry V defeated the French. **1431** Death of Joan of Arc. England gradually loses her land in France. **1450** Wars of the Roses in England.
ASIA AND AFRICA	**1200** Mongols under Genghis Khan began conquest of Asia. They made the only successful winter invasion of Russia in history.	**1275** Marco Polo visits China. Kublai Khan ruled China. Rise of the Ottoman Empire.	**1300** Trade with Africa through the Middle East. Luxury goods and salt were exchanged for gold and slaves.	**1350** Ming dynasty in China with a new capital at Beijing (Peking) It became the most advanced and powerful state in the world, and exported silk and cotton to the West.	**1400** Kingdom of Benin in Africa established. Explorers searched for a sea-route to China and India through the Caribbean.
ARTS AND SCIENCES	**1226** Death of St Francis of Assisi. Great period of building of cathedrals. Age of Gothic architecture. Oxford and Cambridge are universities.	**1250** Age of Great Italian poets, notably Dante and Petrarch. Latin is the professional language of Europe. Islamic architecture reaches India.	**1300** Italians invent spectacles. **1339** The building of the Kremlin in Moscow.	**1350** Aztecs wrote the codices and also developed a complex calendar system.	**1400** Beginning of the Italian Renaissance. Death of Geoffrey Chaucer in England. **1430** The Fortress of Zimbabwe built in Africa. **1445** First book in Europe, The Bible, is printed by Gutenberg.

1450	1500	1520	1550	1600
1487 Great temple of Tenochtitlan consecrated. Many prisoners sacrificed. Aztecs expand southwards into the lands of the Maya. **1500** Moctezuma II elected as Great Speaker.	**1519** Cortes lands in Mexico. Moctezuma killed.	**1521** Tenochtitlan destroyed. **1535** Mexico ruled by a vice-regent for the King of Spain. Tenochtitlan rebuilt as the capital of New Spain. Export of silver to Europe.		
1478 First Russian Tzar (Ivan III). **1492** Christopher Columbus reaches America. **1493** New World divided between Spain and Portugal.			**1550** Naples, Venice, Milan, Constantinople and Paris are the only cities in Europe with more than 100,000 people.	
1498 First European sea voyage to India and back by Vasco de Gama. Spain begins to conquer North Africa.	**1500** Introduction of sugar-cane, rice and citrus fruits into Europe from Asia.		**1550** Mughal dynasty in India. Slaves from Africa reached America.	
1450 Age of great Italian artists. Leonardo da Vinci 1452–1519. Michelangelo 1475–1564. Raphael 1483–1520.	**1500** The potato introduced into Europe from South America.		**1550** First watch invented in Germany. **1559** Tobacco Introduced into Europe from the Americas.	

RULE BY THE AZTECS

Although the Aztecs only arrived in the Valley of Mexico about 1200 AD, two hundred years later they controlled the whole valley.

The rulers of the Aztecs married princesses from other tribes which meant they could trace their ancestors back to the Old Kingdom of the Toltecs who had ruled Mexico hundreds of years before.

However, the Aztecs ruled by force and when the Spaniards arrived, some of the other tribes were happy to fight with Spain against them.

QUOTATIONS

In 1569 a Franciscan missionary Bernadino de Sahagún wrote a *General History of the Things of New Spain* with the help of Aztec nobles. The quotations in this book in bold text are translations from his book.

DID·THE AZTECS GROW·THEIR OWN·FOOD?

The Aztecs began with the worst land in the valley but ended by being almost agriculturally self-sufficient. As the population grew and the city expanded, more and more land was needed to grow food. Land was reclaimed from the lake to make the *chinampas* described below, while in other areas, a system of rotation made sure every field was used to capacity. The dry growing season in January followed a short cold winter, while May to October was hot and wet. All plants were the children of sacred Mother Earth.

FLOATING GARDENS

The *chinampas* below were made by piling up layers of mud and vegetation from the shallow lakes around the city. Held together by tree roots, they provided fertile vegetable gardens. All kinds of crops like tomatoes, squash, and beans as well as flowers were grown all the year round on the fertile soil. Canals between the islands were used like pathways by the farmers.

THE FARMING YEAR

The agricultural year was organized very carefully. There were special days for planting and sowing, weeding and harvesting. All farmers gave some of their produce in tribute and were expected to work hard and honor the gods. "*Labor, sow and plant your trees. Do not cast off your burden or grow faint or be lazy – if you are lazy you will not be able to support your wife and family*." But it was the women and children who weeded the fields and scared away the birds.

TOOLS

The digging stick was the basic tool of the Aztec farmer. Apart from a hoe nothing else was needed to grow and harvest their crops. They did not use a plow or any wheeled vehicles at all. In fact there was little change in farming techniques for some 5000 years.

Digging stick

Hoe

CORN

The most important and basic food was corn. It was eaten every day both as *tortillas* (pancakes) or as a soup. Before planting the grain the farmer talked to the seed and prayed for a good harvest. Without corn the people would starve. Special gods looked after the corn, like Tlaloc who brought rain and made the earth rich. Below you can see Tlaloc blessing the corn plant; it is shown as his young wife with a digging stick in front of her.

DID YOU KNOW?

About 600 sq yards of *chinampa* would support one person.

About 44,000 tons of corn was needed every year to feed the Aztecs' city

Human excrement was collected and used as fertilizer. This system also helped to keep the city clean.

In times of drought plagues of mice and insects appeared. People would sell themselves as slaves to nobles in the hope of extra food.

DID · THE AZTECS EAT · WELL ?

The Aztec diet was based on corn. *Tortillas* or corn pancakes are still eaten in Mexico today, but in the time of the Aztecs corn was much more important. There were few dairy products as there were no native cattle or sheep. Poorer people ate little meat so protein came mainly from beans. The diet may sound dull, but was healthy, with many vegetables then unknown outside Mexico like avocados. At banquets, duck, turkey or even dog was served.

FEASTING
"Listen – above all be careful in food and drink. Do not eat too much. Eat and drink slowly and quietly. Do not stir up the pieces and dig into the bowl!" But food was to be enjoyed and one merchant provided 100 turkeys and 40 dogs in a sauce for his guests. If chillies were not served as well, it was a fast not a feast.

DRINKING
Only the elderly were allowed to get drunk, as you can see above. The punishment for drunkenness was severe – even for a first offence the head was shaved – but it seems that this did not stop people drinking, especially at banquets and festivals. A very special and expensive non-alcoholic drink for the nobility was made from cacao beans. We call it chocolate.

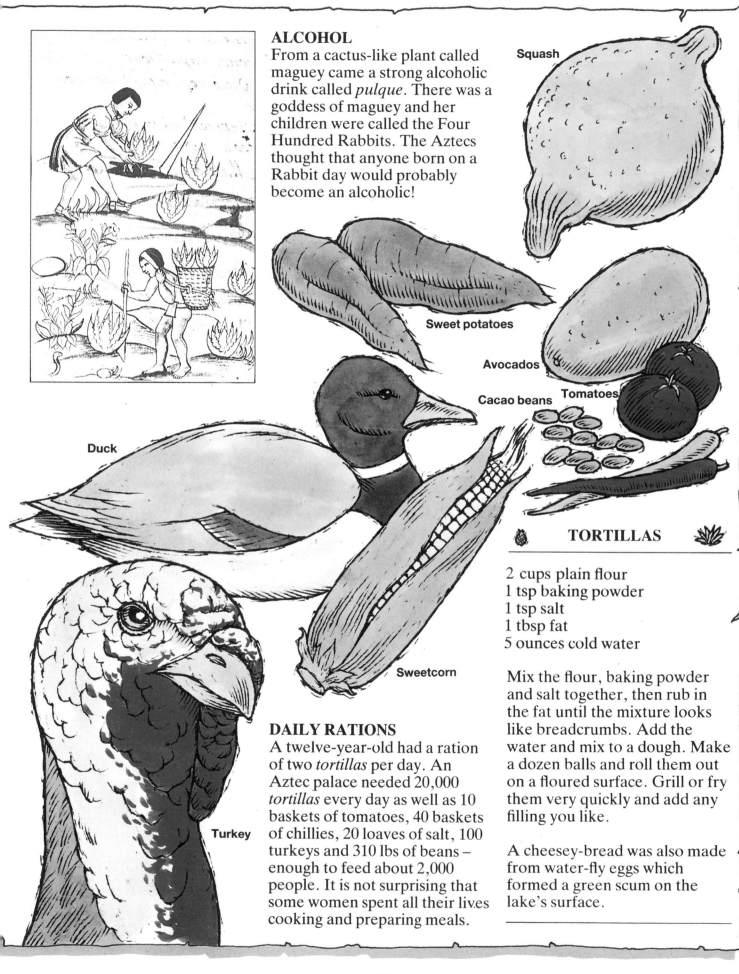

ALCOHOL

From a cactus-like plant called maguey came a strong alcoholic drink called *pulque*. There was a goddess of maguey and her children were called the Four Hundred Rabbits. The Aztecs thought that anyone born on a Rabbit day would probably become an alcoholic!

Squash

Sweet potatoes

Avocados

Cacao beans

Tomatoes

Duck

Sweetcorn

Turkey

DAILY RATIONS

A twelve-year-old had a ration of two *tortillas* per day. An Aztec palace needed 20,000 *tortillas* every day as well as 10 baskets of tomatoes, 40 baskets of chillies, 20 loaves of salt, 100 turkeys and 310 lbs of beans – enough to feed about 2,000 people. It is not surprising that some women spent all their lives cooking and preparing meals.

TORTILLAS

2 cups plain flour
1 tsp baking powder
1 tsp salt
1 tbsp fat
5 ounces cold water

Mix the flour, baking powder and salt together, then rub in the fat until the mixture looks like breadcrumbs. Add the water and mix to a dough. Make a dozen balls and roll them out on a floured surface. Grill or fry them very quickly and add any filling you like.

A cheesey-bread was also made from water-fly eggs which formed a green scum on the lake's surface.

DID · THE AZTECS · HAVE FAMILIES LIKE · OURS?

Marriage and the family were central to Aztec life. If men were honored for fighting in battle then women received equal honor by having children. Ordinary men had one wife, but nobles often married many more for political reasons. Married children sometimes lived with their parents and grandparents who would give lots of advice and organize the household. In-laws were called peacemakers, so perhaps not all the good advice was taken. Children married at about twenty.

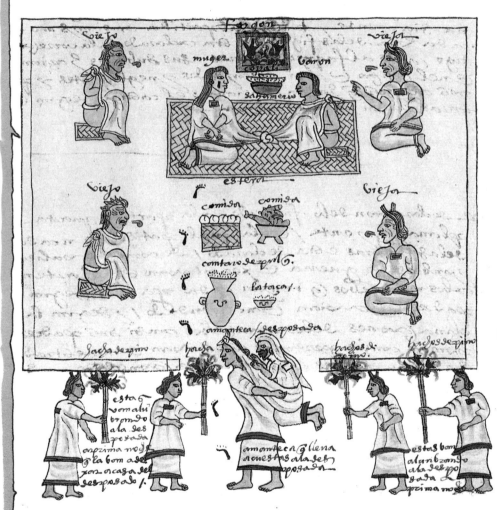

Bow and arrows

Blanket

Loincloth

MARRIAGE
Although marriage was arranged by parents with the help of a matchmaker, the young man and woman had to agree to it. But it was thought very rude for the girl to say 'yes' to a proposal of marriage the first time of asking. As soon as everything was arranged, there was a feast and presents of cloaks and corn were given. Above the bride is carried on the matchmaker's back to the groom's house where their clothes are tied together to symbolize marriage. After four days there was another feast.

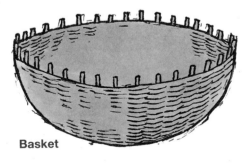

Basket

HOUSEHOLD DUTIES

Women ran the household and all girls were taught to cook and weave, even if some of them had servants to do these things. A girl had to be obedient and pure, and a mother careful and hardworking. Both parents helped to teach their children what was expected of them as adults. A 'good' child was healthy and happy but a 'bad' child was sick and violent. All were trained to be obedient and respectful to older people. Men also had responsibilities outside the home: on the land and in battle for their masters.

CHILDBIRTH

When a baby was born relatives visited with presents and advice. The baby's future was read by an astrologer, then it was bathed and named. A boy was given a tiny shield and arrows; a girl had a spindle whorl and weaving tools. Other children ran about shouting out the child's name such as Miauaxiuitl ('Turquoise Maize Flower'), Quaulicoatl ('Eagle Serpent') or Moctezuma ('Angry Lord').

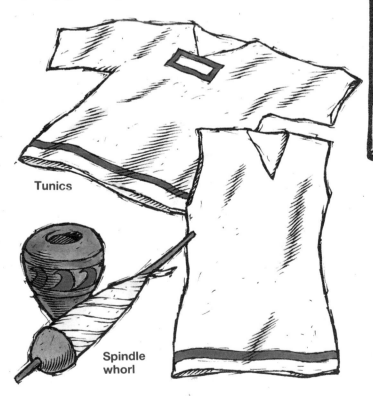

Tunics

Spindle whorl

PREGNANCY

A pregnant woman received a great deal of advice, some of it very sensible:
Do not lift heavy things.
Do not go out at night for fear of spirits.
Do not look at anything red or anything frightening.

If a women died in childbirth she was honored as a goddess.

"When we saw so many great cities and villages built on the water and other great towns built on dry land we were amazed . . . great towers and temples rising from the water and all built of stone. Some of our soldiers asked whether the things we saw were but a dream." So wrote a Spaniard on first seeing the capital city, Tenochtitlan, with its brightly painted temples and palaces joined together by causeways that were wide enough for ten horses. It was the biggest city that they had ever seen.

TENOCHTITLAN

The name of the city means 'Place of the Fruit of the Prickly Pear Cactus'. Planned around a central walled temple area, it had many palaces and baths, law courts, a zoo and a university. On the edges of the city the farmers built temporary thatched huts, but most buildings were made of a soft stone that was easily cut into blocks, plastered and polished.

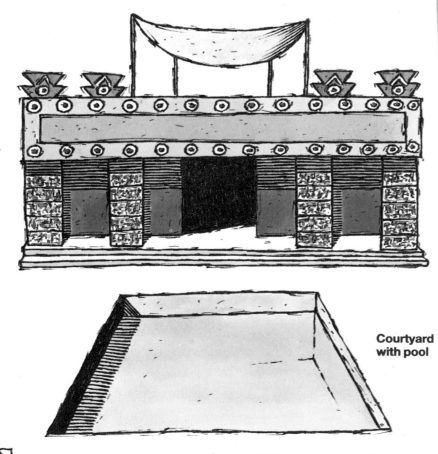

Roof awning for hot weather

Courtyard with pool

HOUSES

Ordinary people lived in a one-roomed house with a square doorway in one wall. The flat roof was used as an extra room in hot weather. Only nobles were allowed two-storey houses. These were usually built around a central courtyard with a pool and lots of flowers, which the Aztecs loved. Each quarter of the city was divided into units or *calpulli* with their own school, temple and 'town hall'.

DAILY LIFE

People spent a lot of time outdoors but went to bed at sunset. Only priests went out at night, for fear of evil spirits. Houses had no windows and doors had no locks as stealing was almost unheard of (thieves could be sold as slaves). There was a good public sanitation service and everyone was expected to keep their streets swept and clean. Indoors it was a girl's job to sweep out the house. The mother on the left is making her daughter work at night as a punishment.

FURNITURE

Houses had very little furniture. Everyone sat and slept on reed mats with just a cotton blanket . . . even in winter. Only noblemen were allowed to sit on the legless chairs as you can see from the wedding picture on page 16. Clothes were kept in wooden boxes and every home had a loom. Pots like these were hand-coiled and decorated by women at home. The two cups are for *pulque*.

THE FIREPLACE

At the center of the house was the sacred hearth where the fire was never allowed to go out. Around it were the three sacred stones in the shape of a triangle with a clay disk on top for cooking. There were little shrines to other gods like Ixtlilton who protected sleeping children and Xilonen who looked after their health.

POPULATION

In 1500 Tenochtitlan was bigger than any city in Europe with a population of about 250,000 within 5–6 square miles.

The whole valley had a population of between 1 and 2 million people.

Many houses had sweatbaths in the courtyard rather like our saunas, which helped to keep the population healthy.

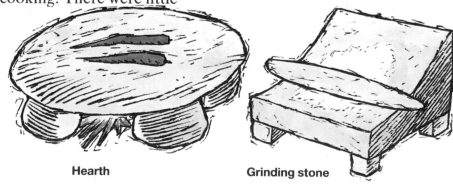

Hearth   **Grinding stone**

· D I D · CHILDREN GO · T O SCHOOL ?

It was important for children to learn how to behave. When they were four, boys helped to carry water and firewood. By six they were learning to fish and take goods to market. Girls were mainly taught at home and began spinning at four and cooking at twelve. Their education was basically a training for marriage, although noble girls spent a year at 12 or 13 helping in the temple, and some became professional priestesses.

WEAVING

"Apply yourself to the really womanly task, the spindle whorl, the weaving stick". Below you can see how the girl's own weight kept the loom tight. Women took little direct part in public life but had a lot of influence behind the scenes.

SCHOOLWORK

At 15 boys went either to the *calmecac* or the *cuicacalli*. The *calmecac* was run by priests who taught religious and administrative subjects, mainly to noble children. The *cuicacalli* was more of a military school. However, all boys were trained in war and there was great rivalry between the schools, which often led to fights. All boys had to work hard on the land too, but the *calmecac* pupils had extra religious duties as well as lessons in history, astronomy, poetry and, what the Aztecs regarded as most important, writing.

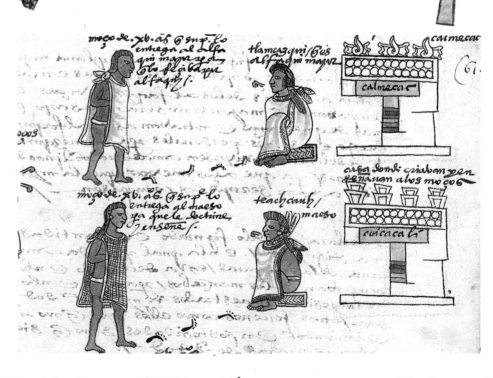

CALMECAC

At the *calmecac* the pupils were pricked with maguey spikes if they fell asleep or did not pay attention. The teachers were warriors as well as priests. All noble boys knew how to fight – "**they took him to the wars . . . they taught him well and made him see how he might take a captive**". Priests gained more status if they captured many prisoners and received the same honors as other fighters. Below are two priests with their prisoners.

PUNISHMENT

Children were told not to be idle and they were warned against the vices of gambling and theft, gossip and drink. Punishment was painful – here an 11-year-old boy (the dots over his head give his age) inhales chilli-pepper smoke while the girl is only threatened.

GOOD MANNERS

There were rules and regulations for everything:
Do not eat fast or smack your lips.
Do not sneeze or spit on someone else's food.
Do not drop food on someone else's clothes.
Do not dress in odd clothes or trip over your cloak.
Do not mock the old, sick or disabled.
Always behave with dignity.

WRITING

The art of writing was very specialized and difficult to learn. There was no alphabet but many glyphs or pictures. These only gave a clue to the full meaning and a scribe needed to know a lot of extra information that was not actually written down. Some glyphs were ideographs (using part to mean the whole) for example footprints meant travel, and a scroll in front of the mouth meant speech.

PICTOGRAMS

Alligator

Flint knife

Snake

Reed

Death

Rabbit

Monkey

Eagle

Jaguar

Deer

Movement

Vulture

Although the basis of Aztec life was agricultural, farmers were so successful and farmed so intensively that it was not necessary for everybody to work on the land and grow food. There were other professions, especially in the arts and crafts, politics, the military as well as the priesthood. There was also another very important group of people – the merchants and traders who organized all the markets and who held a special place in Aztec society.

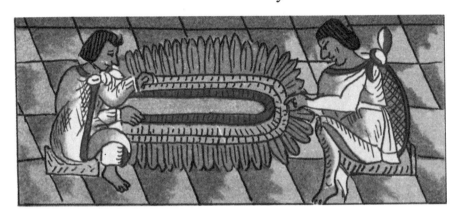

CRAFTWORKERS

Craftworkers organized themselves into guilds to protect their trade. They had their own areas of the city and passed their skills on from parent to child, both boys and girls. On the right an apprentice is learning about stone carving, polishing and featherworking. On the left you can see skilled featherworking. Parents asked the gods that a girl "*might dye things well . . . might tint rabbit fur . . . dye feathers . . . judge colors so she can work her feathers.*" There was a careful division of work. Women sorted and dyed and children made up the glue while men prepared the backing and stuck on the feathers.

MERCHANTS

Yacatecuhtli or 'Lord Nose' was the god of merchants. Here he carries a crossroads with four footprints to symbolize long journeys. Behind him a trader with his staff and fan carries quetzal birds. Even rich merchants did not show their wealth in public but always dressed simply.

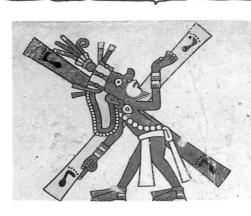

METALWORKERS

Gold and metalworkers made jewelery and beautiful objects for the nobility, such as birds with moving wings and even dancing monkeys. Silver and gold were mined in the mountains and reached the city either by trade or tribute. Every piece of this work was unique as the mold had to be broken when the metal was cast. Jade was thought to be more precious than gold and a skilled lapidary (stoneworker) was highly thought of. Goldsmiths also had their own god, Xipe Totec (see page 29).

PAY

There was no actual money. Aztecs used cacao beans for trade if necessary.

Full-time artists worked in the palaces. Before work, they were paid 10 loads of squash, 10 loads of beans, 2 loads of chillies, cacao and cotton. On completion they were paid 2 slaves, 2 loads of cacao, pottery, salt and more clothing.

Quetzal feathers

Jaguar skin

IDEALS

Not everybody worked as hard as they should have done. We know of lazy farmers, careless artists, cheating merchants and lying traders. We also know of faking cacao beans, hiding cheap cotton inside expensive bales and selling moldy chillies, even though these activities were illegal. There were other professions in this complex and bureaucratic society such as doctors and astrologers, scribes and gamblers; everyone had something to do.

WHAT·DID THEY·DO·IN ·THEIR· SPARE·TIME?

Although people were constantly reminded about the virtues of hard work there seems to have been spare time for games, feasts and religious festivals. Life could be hard and uncertain, so the gods had to be constantly honored by sacrifice and thanksgiving. Every three weeks there were calendar festivals and day festivals for different occupations. Merchants gave the best banquets with tubes of tobacco (unknown in Europe), food, chocolate and special mushrooms which gave the guests hallucinations.

AZTEC BACKGAMMON

Patolli was one of the most popular games of all and was played rather like backgammon. Four cacao beans painted with white dots for numbers were the dice. Each player moved six pebble counters along the board. Professional players carried their dice wrapped in cloth and talked to them before a game.

Players gambled everything on the game – clothes, feathers, fields, houses and even their children. Some sold themselves as slaves when they had no more to lose.

Two-tone drum

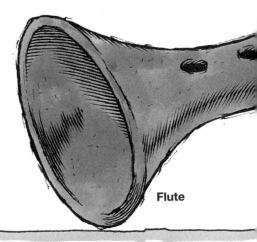

Flute

24

HATCHLI

Hundreds of years before the Aztecs arrived people had played a ball-game called *hatchli* or *tlatchli*. It needed a court which could be 65 yards long with rings on either side. Most temples had a ball-court attached to them and the game had a ritual meaning as well as entertainment value. The players could only use their hips and knees to get the ball through the rings. The ball was so hard they wore padded hip-guards, but players were often badly bruised and sometimes killed.

MUSIC

Music with a strong rhythmic beat was important at banquets and festivals. The *teponaztli* or two-tone drum has two flaps at the top to make the sound. Whistles helped dancers keep time while children played simple flutes and ocarinas. Everyone joined in the singing and dancing.

Whistle

PLAYS AND POEMS

The Aztecs had a strong tradition of plays, poems and histories. Children learned popular songs and sagas by heart. People's deepest fears and highest hopes were expressed in poetry. " . . . *each spring brings us life,*
The golden corn refreshes us,
The pink corn makes us a necklace.
At least this we know –
The hearts of our friends are true."

FESTIVALS AND HOLIDAYS

Every morning thanks were given to the gods for being alive – people pricked their ears and offered two drops of blood.

In July to August there was a flower festival; in September came harvest and cleaning houses and temples; October had the hunting festival. Every festival demanded human sacrifice, even of children.

There was time for hunting and fishing for both food and pleasure.

Gardening was popular too, but some people just sat around and enjoyed gossip.

Whistle

Ocarina

· W H A T ·
D I D · T H E
A Z T E C S
· W E A R ? ·

The status of every Aztec was known by what they wore and their hair-style. It was a serious offence to wear clothes that you were not entitled to. Ordinary people wore cloth made from maguey (cactus) fiber; only nobles were allowed to wear cotton and even this privilege could be taken away if they broke the law. The basic dress for all men was just a simple loin-cloth knotted in front and a cloak knotted on the shoulder. The higher the status, the more expensive and highly decorated the clothing.

HEADDRESSES

This headdress may have belonged to the ruler Moctezuma himself. It is made of green quetzal feathers and blue Cotinga feathers, together with gold and turquoise. We know that many luxurious presents like this were sent to the King of Spain and this may have been one of them.

TURQUOISE JEWELERY

This pendant may also have been part of the treasure sent to the Spanish invaders. The double-headed serpent was a symbol of the rain god Tlaloc. It is made of hollow wood to make it lighter to wear and could be worn either as part of a headdress or as a pendant. It is covered in turquoise mosaic with red and white shell inlay. Such skilled work was seen as a gift from the god Quetzalcoatl.

WOMEN'S DRESS

Women wore plain wrap-around skirts that came below the knee and overtunics like ponchos that were often brightly embroidered and fringed. Here is Lady Precious Green, the young wife of the god Tlaloc, squatting on her heels as all Aztec women did. Her hair is loose under her headdress but with two plaits at the back. Most married women wound their plaits round their head leaving the two ends sticking up like horns. Both sexes painted their faces.

Pendant

GOLD AND JADE

The Aztecs preferred jade to gold as green was the ideal color, but men and women wore gold earrings as well as nose plugs. Rich nobles even pierced their lower lips and hung pendants from them.

Ordinary people were not allowed such luxuries, but a small jade pendant was given to a new baby as a good luck charm.

Ear plug

Nose plug

Nose plug

Lip plug

HYGIENE

Girls washed, combed and oiled their hair. Priests did not wash or cut their hair at all so it was full of insects and smelt.
Boys grew a long tuft of hair on the back of their heads until they had captured their first prisoner. It was an insult to call anyone "big tuft of hair on the back of the head".
Girls had to be careful not to show their knees or their breasts as they walked.

CLOAKS

Unless you were a noble or had battle scars on your legs, it was illegal to wear a long cloak below the knee. You could be killed if you were caught. However, the man on the right is a commander of warriors and is quite entitled to his long cloak and the quetzal feathers in his headdress. It shows that he has captured many prisoners and done many brave deeds.

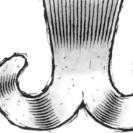

WHO·DID·THE·AZTECS·WORSHIP?

Although we can describe the ceremonies and rituals of the Aztecs, we do not know what they really thought. There was a god for every aspect of human life. Some gods had many different names and functions. From the beginning of time the Aztecs believed that there had been four previous worlds which had been destroyed by jaguars, wind, fire and water. They believed their world, the fifth world, would be destroyed by earthquakes and only human sacrifices kept the sun rising every day.

THE EARTH MOTHER

This is one of a pair of statues from the Great Temple in Tenochtitlan. It was found in 1824 buried in front of the 'modern' cathedral. It is Coatlicue, 'Great Lady of the Serpent Skirt and Earth Mother'. She stands for the pain of life itself with her skirt of serpents (poverty), her claws (digging), her heart necklace (pain of life) and skull, reminding people that they too return to the earth.

TEZCATLIPOCA

He is always recognizable because of his missing foot which was eaten by the earth monster as he dragged the world from the waters, before humans were created. He is 'Smoking Mirror', the dark side of life, the god of magic, war and death, who was in endless conflict with Quetzalcoatl. Together they symbolized both sides of human nature.

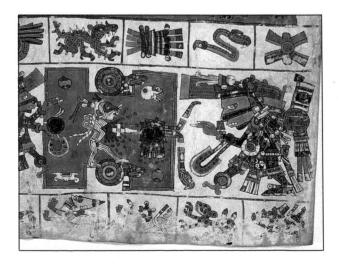

SKULL RACKS

Skull racks or *tzompantli* were found in every temple for all to see. The skulls were threaded on to poles after sacrifice and left to rot. It was said that there were more than 10,000 on one rack alone. But without such sacrifice they believed that the world would end.

XIPE TOTEC

The god of spring and new life was also the god of suffering. He wears a human skin, for at his festival a prisoner was skinned alive and the skin worn by the priests to show the new life bursting from the old. He has his eyes closed in death, and once held a rattle in each hand.

Skull rack

PLACES OF WORSHIP

The Aztecs built temples to all their gods, from the great creator and fertility gods of the state to the local gods they had adopted as their own from the previous inhabitants of the valley. Every house had its own little altar but at festivals the people came to the temple to take part in public services. Sacrifices took place at the top of the steep staircase where all could see.

GODS

Gods were recognized by their different headdresses and colors.

Xochipilli – Prince of Flowers, god of dawn, the ball-game, dance and love. Shown as eternally young, wearing flowered sandals and painted red.

Huehueteotl – god of fire. Shown as a toothless old man.

Tloque Nahuaque – lord of everywhere. The one supreme force, both male and female.

DID·THEY BELIEVE·IN LIFE·AFTER DEATH?

There was a life after death, but what happened depended more on the way you died than on your behavior in life. There were special burial ceremonies for 'fortunate' people like merchants, or for anyone who had drowned, women who had died in childbirth, and most especially for warriors and those who had been sacrificed. But most people were cremated and went to Mictlan, the gloomy underworld, which they reached after a long journey and many difficulties.

THE GOD QUETZALCOATL
This mask made of turquoise and shell with a blue and a green serpent twisting around the eyes is the god Quetzalcoatl. He was the Lord of Life who created mankind and Lord of the Winds who brought fertility and new life. His name means both 'feathered' and 'precious serpent'. Aztec legends tell of how he was once a king on earth but sacrificed himself for his people to become the Morning Star and bringer of life. He is the intelligent and conscious side of human beings and quite different from the evil spirits who might return from the dead to capture children or frighten them with nightmares.

AFTER DEATH

This sacrificial knife is made from obsidian, or volcanic glass. The handle shows an eagle-warrior. After four years, dead warriors and sacrificial victims came back to earth as humming-birds or butterflies.

A MERCHANT'S BURIAL

The merchant below has died. His body is wrapped-up carefully and decorated with feathers and paper ornaments. His possessions surround him – gold, precious stones, feathers and jaguar skins. These will be buried with him. His friends will sing sad songs and hold a great feast in his honor.

LORD OF THE DEAD

On the journey to Mictlan, the underworld, the dead passed through the Wind of Knives which cut all the flesh from their bones. Living skeletons feasted and danced at the court of the Lord of the Dead. There is still a Day of the Dead in Mexico when people decorate everything with skulls and skeletons.

Totona pottery figure

SACRIFICE

The Aztecs believed that human sacrifice kept the world alive. The gods needed blood.

The usual method of sacrifice was to have the heart cut out.

Children were drowned and their tears were considered a good omen for rain in the spring – even though spring was the

time of year when it rained naturally anyway.

A girl was beheaded at the corn festival and her blood brought good crops. No one knew who would be chosen for the sacrifice.

Some prisoners were drugged and then skinned alive.

· W H O · RULED · THE AZTECS ?

The center of Aztec government was the city-state with each one ruled by a Great Speaker, but by 1500 the city of Tenochtitlan was the most important and all other cities paid it tribute. In the beginning, the Great Speaker had been elected by all the Aztecs but eventually the position belonged to just one family and the best candidate was chosen. Aztec society was like a pyramid, with the Great Speaker as ruler at the top and many slaves at the bottom.

NOBLES AND COMMONERS

The most important social division was between nobles and commoners. This was determined by birth, for nobles had to trace their family back to the first Aztec ruler, through either of their parents, and so back to the god Quetzalcoatl himself. Here are three high-ranking military officials (it was possible to rise in society through bravery in battle).

Commoners were called *macehualli*, 'the Chosen Ones', and they organized themselves into clans or *calpulli* (which means 'big house'). Each *calpulli* owned land which was given out to all its members. Slaves did much of the hard work on the nobles' lands. They were usually prisoners taken in battle, criminals or gamblers.

THE GREAT SPEAKERS

Every Great Speaker had a special way of writing his name. Here are all the names of these Aztec rulers. Moctezuma's was a crowned head while his uncle Ahuitzotl had a long-tailed animal as his sign. You can see him again on the stone box below, which may be part of his coffin.

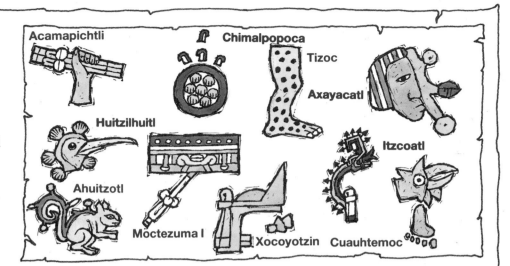

Acamapichtli

Chimalpopoca

Tizoc

Axayacatl

Huitzilhuitl

Itzcoatl

Ahuitzotl

Moctezuma I

Xocoyotzin

Cuauhtemoc

DUTIES OF THE RULER

The ruler had responsibility for his people and the defense of his city, but every new reign began with a war. The Great Speaker had to capture many prisoners, who were sacrificed to the gods at his coronation. Ahuitzotl was a great warrior who extended the empire and the Great Temple. When he dedicated a new temple to the gods, more than 4,000 people were sacrificed.

SERVANTS OF THE EMPIRE

"Everything was so well-recorded that no detail was left out of the account. There were even officials in charge of sweeping". But all were supported by the state, so more and more wars were needed to feed and clothe them. It became a vicious circle. Wealth honored the gods who gave more victories, which meant greater ceremonies. It is no wonder that temples collapsing in flames were the symbols of conquest.

 LAWS

Every city-state had its own law courts, and judges had to be completely fair and never take bribes. Lying to the court was lying to the gods. The penalty was death! Anyone could go to court but nobles often got harsher punishments as they should have known better and set an example. It was death if tax-collectors took too much or if anyone disobeyed in battle.

WERE·THERE ANY·AZTEC ARTISTS?

The Aztecs had no special word for art or artists. Artistic skills were a gift from god and art was in the service of the gods. Artists were admired by all and a certain amount of artistic training was usual for everyone, however noble. As many people could not read or write, ideas, usually religious, were explained in a visual way through sculpture, painting and symbols. Since the glory was the gods', and not man's, artists did not sign their work.

GIANT SCULPTURES

No one had made so many and such large sculptures before. Some were over 7 feet high and stood in the temples. Every god had its own special symbols and colors, and it is difficult to tell who was who as all the colors have gone. But the teeth and mouth of Tlaloc make him easy to recognize.

CHACMOOLS

The Aztecs borrowed many of their artistic traditions from previous peoples who had lived in the valley, especially the Toltecs who had ruled hundreds of years before. These stone figures are called Chacmools and often stood at the entrance to both Toltec and Aztec temples. The bowl on their stomach was for blood and offerings, often to the rain god Tlaloc. Originally they were very brightly painted, like the temples and houses.

ANIMAL ART

The snake is the most common animal in Aztec art and one of the most sacred as it was associated with the Earth and fertility as well as the gods. Its name, *coatl*, is found in the names of several gods. Some carvings are very lifelike, but others are more symbolic, like the snake-heads carved around the outside walls of temples and up the huge stairways. Live snakes were kept in jars filled with feathers to breed.

FEATHERWORKERS

Featherworking was a traditional craft using both common birds like the turkey and heron and the more exotic quetzal, Cotinga and parrot. The finished feather mosaic was so fine it looked almost like a painting. A paper pattern was cut out and stuck to prepared cotton to form a stencil. Then it was transferred to a backing and the feathers stuck on one by one starting with the cheapest, which were often dyed to make them look like the exotic green quetzal feathers. For cloaks and shirts the feathers were sewn on to the cloth to make a brilliant mosaic pattern.

COLORS

Aztec painters used natural colors and did not mix them.
Red – from cochineal (an insect dye).
Green – from vegetable dye.
Blue – they used chalk (dyed with flowers).
Yellow – from ochre.
Purple – from shellfish (as the Romans did).
Everything was outlined in black on a white background.

PAINTERS

A *tlacuilo* or 'putter down of thoughts' was highly respected in Aztec society. Books or codices were called 'thought paintings' and were made of long strips of deer-skin about 8 inches wide. These were folded like a concertina and might be up to about 20 feet long with paintings on both sides. Lines marked out the figures which were painted without shading onto the limewashed surface.

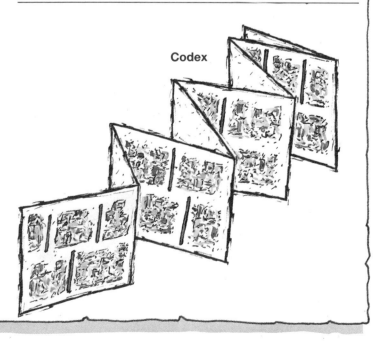

Codex

DID·THEY ·USE· TECHNOLOGY?

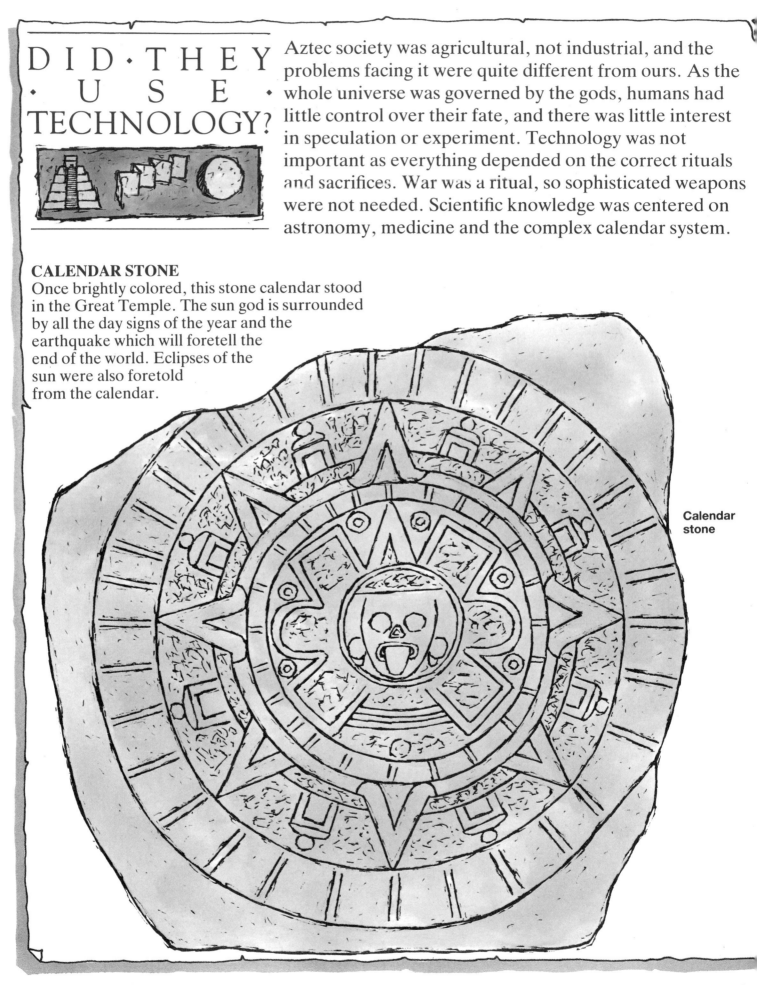

Aztec society was agricultural, not industrial, and the problems facing it were quite different from ours. As the whole universe was governed by the gods, humans had little control over their fate, and there was little interest in speculation or experiment. Technology was not important as everything depended on the correct rituals and sacrifices. War was a ritual, so sophisticated weapons were not needed. Scientific knowledge was centered on astronomy, medicine and the complex calendar system.

CALENDAR STONE
Once brightly colored, this stone calendar stood in the Great Temple. The sun god is surrounded by all the day signs of the year and the earthquake which will foretell the end of the world. Eclipses of the sun were also foretold from the calendar.

Calendar stone

ASTRONOMY

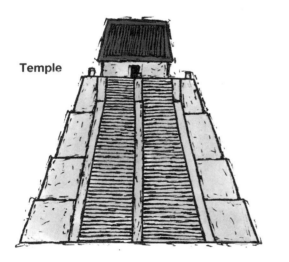

Temple

The year was divided into 365 days with 18 months of 20 days each. The spare five days were thought to be unlucky.

The sacred calendar had 260 days of 20 months of 13 days each.

The two calendars made an important 52-year cycle.

Aztec astronomers had calculated the orbit of Venus and Mars by watching the stars.

MEDICINE

An Aztec doctor was very practical and had "*a knowledge of herbs . . . experience . . . prudence . . . he provides health, restores people, provides them with splints . . . makes incisions, stitches them, revives them*". They used many herbal remedies both to cure and prevent illness, and understood a great deal about the human body. With war and sacrifices there were plenty of bodies to practice on.

"*We must continue to march onwards.*" The Aztecs had started out as a nomadic people wandering from place to place, but once settled on Lake Texcoco they preferred to stay there. People did not travel for its own sake. Those who traveled most were merchants, the porters they hired for every expedition, and warriors. Some had even seen the sea.

SEA TRAVEL
This canoe is filled with Aztecs in preparation for battle against the Spaniards.

PORTERS
Here is the god Quetzalcoatl shown as a typical porter carrying corn on his back with a strap round his forehead. This is how most goods were carried across the 'empire', as there were no horses or carts. The mountains and forests were covered in narrow tracks. Porters jogged between cities, usually with bare feet, carrying up to 90 lbs on their backs. What was not carried this way went by water in a simple dug-out canoe made from a single tree-trunk.

MERCHANT TRAVELERS
Without the merchants or *pochteca*, the Aztec economy would have collapsed. But at home the merchants seemed humble and poor, and crept quietly back to their houses, even if their expeditions had been successful: ". . . *not by day, but by night they swiftly entered by boat . . . then swiftly he took away his boat. When it dawned, nothing remained*."

However, their wealth went on expensive feasts to impress other members of their profession. A young trader "*must first feel and profit by the pain, the afflictions . . . the ambushes. Such is exacted from those who go from city to city . . . you will be in danger . You will shed tears*."

But there were rewards too, and by 1500 the merchants were almost rivaling the nobles in wealth and power.

SOLDIERS

Here is a young priest going off to war with his porter carrying his kit. But it was merchants, not the army, who first brought back the news of strangers arriving with great 'winged birds'. These were the Spanish galleons – the Aztecs had never seen sailing ships before.

TREASURE

Experts think that this ceremonial shield once belonged to Ahuitzotl (Moctezuma's uncle). It has his sign of the water beast outlined in gold surrounded by feathers. Finding treasure like this made the Spaniards greedy for more and led to the overthrow of the Aztecs.

MARKETS

The market was a very important place in any town. It was where traders met, bartered their goods and swapped stories and information (merchants were also government spies). Even Europeans who had been to Rome and Constantinople had never seen such big and bustling markets. People came in from the countryside to trade with copper axe-blades or jade beads. Each area specialized in local goods and traveling merchants all tried to buy cheaply and sell expensively.

Dugout canoe

RATES OF EXCHANGE

Money was in the form of cacao beans, cotton cloaks, quills of gold dust or copper bells.
For example:

1 pine-bark strip could be exchanged for 1 egg and 2 cacao beans.

DID·THE AZTECS HAVE·AN ·ARMY?·

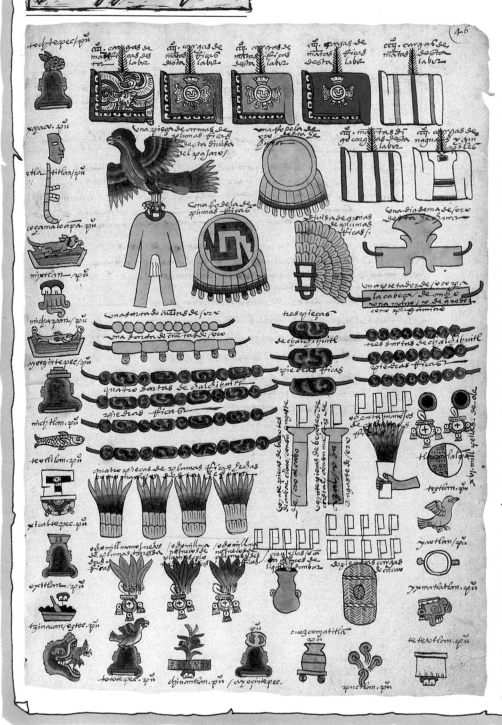

Without wars the Aztec state would have collapsed. War brought land, people and more resources to an ever-expanding population. There was no professional army, although there were professional military officers. Soldiers were ordinary people, for every boy was trained to fight and a boy only became a man after he had captured his first prisoner. War was a duty for the honor of the gods. Living prisoners were most important as they could be fattened-up for sacrifices.

TRIBUTE

Tenochtitlan was not a self-sufficient city. It needed outside help to survive and most of this help came through enforced gifts or tributes of both food and luxury goods. Think of all the different things one coastal province provided in a single year – nearly 10,000 cloaks, 2,000 tunics, a gold shield, gold and jade necklaces, 40 lip-plugs, 80 bunches of quetzal feathers, 16,000 rubber balls (burned as an offering) and 20 sacks of cacao. This is just from one province. If tribute was refused then that area was punished and the tribute was doubled and made more difficult – the Aztecs might ask for live snakes and double-size cloaks. Any slight insult was a good excuse for a fight, with exaggerated demands and furious answers, "*Are you drunk? Are you out of your minds that you've come here with such a demand. Go home . . .*". So they did, but returned with the army and another city was added to the tribute list. All warfare was very highly organized, almost a ritual. The conquered towns were not really destroyed as they were needed to produce the tribute to reward the warriors.

SACRIFICE

Pre-arranged battles or 'wars of the flowers' were sometimes fought for religious purposes. Men were needed for sacrifice. It was an honor to be sacrificed and die as a god. Soldiers sometimes demanded death as their right once they had been captured. A soldier became part of the family and was treated as a son by his captors until the time came for the priest to cut out his heart. By dying victims had made sure that the sun continued to rise, the crops to grow and the land to flourish.

Clubs

SPIES

Spying was very important in wartime. Merchants who knew the country well disguised themselves as peasants and listened to the marketplace gossip. We even know of spies tunneling under an enemy camp in order to listen for any information.

Spears

TAKING PRISONERS

The warrior's costume on the left shows that he has taken many prisoners in battle already.

WEAPONS

Weapons were simple: a circular shield, with a long fringe to keep darts away; obsidian or flint-tipped throwing spears; a throw stick which gave more power to the spear; and a lethal flint-bladed club. Tactics did not change in hundreds of years and no one seems to have bothered to invent anything new.

CANNIBALISM

The palm of the hand was a special delicacy.

Arms and legs of sacrificial victims were cut off, stewed and eaten by the captor's relatives. It was very rude to eat your own prisoners (but you could eat someone else's).

The rest of the body was fed to the animals in the zoo.

· W H A T · HAPPENED TO · THE AZTECS ?

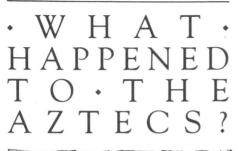

While the Aztecs were expanding their lands, other people across the Atlantic ocean were doing the same. Expeditions from Spain had reached the Caribbean and rumors had been heard of a great civilization on the mainland, full of treasure. The Great Speaker, Moctezuma, was worried when he heard of the strangers. There had been many evil omens foretelling the end of the fifth world and the return of the god, Quetzalcoatl. He wondered if the Spanish leader, Cortes, might be the god himself.

SPANISH CONQUEST

Cortes landed on the coast with about 350 men and 15 horses which the Aztecs had never seen before. It was Good Friday, 1519, and it was also Quetzalcoatl's birthday. Moctezuma soon realized that Cortes was not a god, but the people were still afraid, *"we are already bound to perish. Yes, we can only await death"*. Eventually, the two leaders met and almost became friends.

COLLAPSE AND DESTRUCTION

While Cortes had gone to get more troops many Aztec nobles and priests were murdered. Moctezuma was killed too, probably by Spaniards. Although the troops retreated and many were drowned, the war was really over. The Spaniards returned to destroy Tenochtitlan, house by house. The temple was burned and the images of the gods broken. Smallpox swiftly spread among the Aztecs.

RESULT

In 50 years, the population fell from between 12 and 15 million to 1 million.

Tenochtitlan was flattened. The Great Temple ruins were blown-up and a new cathedral built on them. Spain converted the people to Christianity, so the old culture with its human sacrifices gradually died.

Modern Mexico City (shown below) is built on the same site as Tenochtitlan.

·GLOSSARY·

ANAHUAC 'The Land between the Waters' was the Aztecs' name for their land.

BARTERING Buying and selling through exchange without money.

CACAO BEANS Beans used nowadays for chocolate and cocoa. The Aztecs put a high value on them, and used them to make a special drink.

CALPULLI Groups of families each with their own temple and school.

CHINAMPAS Highly fertile gardens created by the Aztecs in the shallow lakes around their settlements. They were made by piling up silt and rotting vegetation.

CODEX (plural CODICES) Brightly painted manuscripts usually of religious or historical nature. The surviving Aztec codices provide us with a lot of historical evidence.

GREAT SPEAKER The ruler of the Aztecs.

HUITZILOPOCHTLI The tribal god of the Aztecs.

MACEHUALLI Originally meant 'the Chosen Ones'. It came to mean, however, all men and women.

MICTLAN The underworld where most people went after death. Those who did not go to the underworld went to paradise. They included sacrificial victims and women who died in childbirth.

NAHUATL The language of the Aztecs. Nahuatl is related to North American Indian languages.

OBSIDIAN A volcanic glass used for mirrors and sharp-tipped weapons.

OCARINA Wind instrument, often egg-shaped, with mouthpiece and finger holes.

PICTOGRAM A symbol used to represent a word.

PULQUE An alcoholic drink made from the maguey plant (a kind of cactus).

PYRAMID A sloping-sided building, usually a temple.

QUETZAL Brightly colored long-tailed bird whose feathers were used by the Aztecs in their art and dress. it still lives today in the forests of Central America.

QUETZALCOATL The 'good' Aztec god who was also called the Lord of Life and the Lord of the Winds.

SQUASH A vegetable like a marrow or a gourd.

TLALOC 'He Who Makes Things Grow'; a very ancient rain and water god.

TORTILLA A flat corn pancake, the basic food of the Aztecs.

TRIBUTE Gifts of food and goods which the Aztecs extracted from the people they conquered.

TZOMPANTLI The skull-racks where the skulls of sacrificed victims were displayed.

· I N D E X ·